Women & Simple Truths
by
Detroit T. Flanagan, Jr.

To Janis,
Enjoy!
Detroit T. Flanagan Jr.
2-28-95

D1617181

Published by:
ATEA Publishing Company
Los Angeles, CA

&

Wanda Wallace Associates,
Baldwin Hills Crenshaw Plaza
Los Angeles, CA

ACKNOWLEDGEMENTS

The catalogue of people to be thanked for their encouragement, support and love is too numerous to list. So I will collectively say *Thank You* to my many friends and acquaintances who said encouraging words or gave approving nods after having read a poem, or who just said "keep going" when I would rather have stopped.

There are some people whose contribution to this inaugural collection cannot go unspecified. To my wonderful wife, Trula, whose friendship, love, devotion and dedication continue to inspire and excite me after more than 30 years of marriage. Trula, I simply say, "I'm still crazy for you after all these years." To my two precious daughters, Cherice Monai and Dana Lynn, thank you for being the caring, intrepid, dynamic and beautiful young ladies you are. Dad, Detroit Sr., thanks for your constant encouragement. I've never seen you fearful of anything and I thank you for that much-needed example of African-American manhood. To my mother, Naomi, promoted to Glory in 1990, I love you for your inquisitive, gentle, compassionate manner. I know you are smiling on "Junior." My 13 brothers and sisters, I love you all and thank you for the magnificent variety of personalities, talents and challenges you have brought into my life. Your words of assurance have meant a great deal to me in this endeavor. A very special thanks goes to my brother, Jerry Flanagan Black. Your considerable artistic talents and sensitive pictorial interpretations have given my words a special uniqueness.

To the scores already enjoying my works in their bookmark, print and framed forms I thank you with all my heart for embracing these interpretive expressions of God's wisdom. To God Be The Glory

Cover designed by Stuart Sarbone and Detroit Flanagan, Jr.
Edited by Yvonne D. Lewis - Precision Printing & Stationery
Artwork by Jerry Flanagan Black
Author's Photo by Clarence Harley

Published by: ATEA Publishing Company, 3870 Crenshaw Boulevard, #104-425B, Los Angeles, CA 90008 U.S.A. and Wanda Wallace Associates, Fine Art Gallery, Baldwin Hills-Crenshaw Plaza, Los Angeles, CA 90008 U.S.A.

© 1994 by Detroit T. Flanagan, First Printing 1994, First Edition, November 1994

Publisher's Cataloging in Publication Data: Flanagan, Jr., Detroit T.
Women & Simple Truths/ by Detroit T. Flanagan, Jr. - 1st Edition

1. Poetry-General Life   2. Women-Expectations, relationships, etc.
3. Proverbs-Life, love, family, etc.   4. Afro-American-Relationships, etc.

Library of Congress Catalog Card Number: 94-73249
ISBN 0-9644273-3-8 $9.95 Softcover

Table of Contents

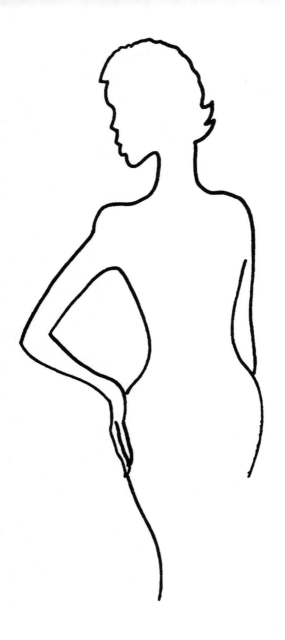

Don't come to me with nothing
cause my stuff you ain't gonna git...

Don't Bring Me No Problems

Don't bring me no problems
I've got plenty of my own
If all you've got are problems
I'd rather be alone

I only have a little
And I worked for every bit
Don't come to me with nothing
Cause my stuff you ain't gonna git

You can be my friend
And perhaps my lover too
But moving in with nothing
Is one thing you'll never do

I'm a woman who needs love
But Mom said long ago
If you let him in with nothing
You can never make him go

So have yourself together
Or don't even look my way
I sure don't need your problems
I can hardly find my way

I don't want him perfect cause
then he won't want me...

I Only Want A Good Man

Why a good man is so hard to find
I can hardly see
I only want him handsome, rich and famous
And crazy about me

On the strictly serious side
I'm not asking for too much
A man with healthy self-respect
And a gentle loving touch

He'll have to have a job of course
A means to pay the rent
And sense enough to save some dough
Each month before it's spent

I'm looking for a caring man
Who'll think enough of me
To give me his encouragement
To be all I can be

I don't want him perfect
Cause then he won't want me
But he must have some common sense
No need for Ph.D.

Maturity and cleanliness
Are things I must demand
If he would be my king
And we walk hand in hand

I only want a good man
One who'll treat me right
Who'll love, protect and cherish me
And woo me day and night

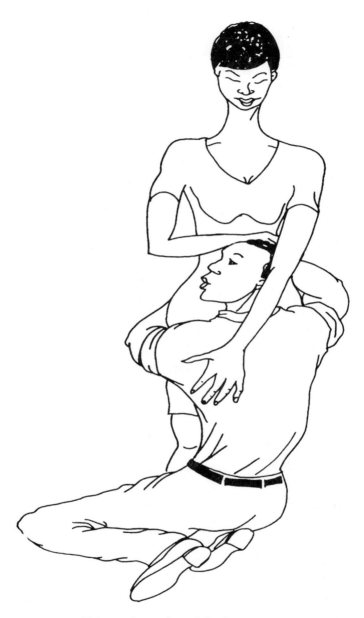

I'd much prefer a black man over
any other kind, but he must be productive...

Black Woman To Black Man

Black man be a man for me
I know you've had it rough
The system's built to keep you down
But you must still be tough

With education lacking
The road is all uphill
I've stood beside you all these years
I'm standing by you still

I'd much prefer a Black man
Over any other kind
But he must be productive
Considerate and kind

Don't keep me waiting Black man
It's time that you mature
This waiting's getting old now
How long must I endure?

If respect is what you want
you must earn it and no fakin...

Bring Home The Bacon

Bring home the bacon
It's a most important thing
Bring home the bacon
If at home you would be king

If respect is what you want
You must earn it and no fakin
Love your family, protect and guide them
And for sure, bring home the bacon

My love for you is boundless
My respect for you quite strong
But don't fail me in the basics
I might have to say "so long"

Give me love because I need it
Kiss me deep when I awaken
Be the man, I know you can
And don't forget, bring home the bacon

I see men who yell at women
I see some who hit them too...

Learning Places

I'd like to pose a question
I'm looking for direction
What makes a man a man?
Please answer if you can

I'm only ten years old
I've never known my dad
A strong, loving mother is
The only role model I've had

I see men who yell at women
I see some who hit them too
When I grow up to be a man
Is that what I should do?

I think instead, when I grow up
I'll do what's taught in school
Be kind and thoughtful toward others
And follow the Golden Rule

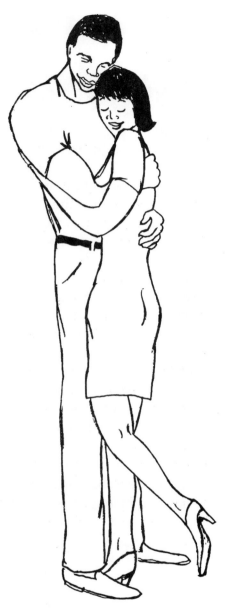

There's nothing that two folks
in love can't work out if they try...

The Right Man

Young lady, look for a man
Who wants to take good care of you
He may not always get it done
But he'll be trying to

Once you have a good thing
Don't kill it with your mouth
Don't tear him down at every chance
Or he just might go south

There's nothing that two folks in love
Can't work out if they try
If either of the two lacks love
Then darlin, say goodbye

The sweetest joy you'll ever know
Is finding someone true
A lover, friend and confidant
Who knows he loves just you

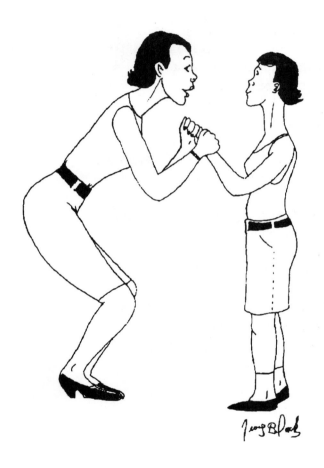

Don't follow your friends wishes
its your life that's at stake...

Advice To A Daughter

To my precious daughter
I have some things to say
I know you might not listen
But I'll say them anyway

The world is full of people
With ideas of every kind
Some ideas will help you
Some put you in a bind

Some ideas can set you back
And cause a little pain
Some can devastate your life
I'm talking to you plain

The challenge for you daughter
Is to differentiate
To tell ideas to cling to
From ideas to hate

The choices won't be easy
But still you'll have to choose
Just follow your own conscience
And you will seldom lose

Don't follow your friend's wishes
It's your life that's at stake
You be the one to choose the path
You say which road you'll take

I'll try to live good values
Since more is caught than taught
So when you have tough choices
You'll do the things you ought

That's it in a nutshell
No soapbox will I mount
Enjoy your life, learn all you can
And please, make your life count.

Who are these children anyway...
These fugitives from pain

Children Of The Night

We hardly pay attention
Or scarcely know they're there
Their plight is not our business
It's just not our affair

Who are these children anyway
What are they out to gain
Runaways, castaways,
These fugitives from pain

They're on the streets, these little ones
Caught up in the storm
Being used, often abused
Lives twisted from the norm

Is there any hope for them?
My heart does truly bleed
To see them caught up hopelessly
So desperately in need

Will no one help, will no one come
To mediate their pain
Why not let your life touch theirs
You both have much to gain

Why do children die each day for want
of love and care?...

Parents Do Your Part

Why do children die each day
For want of love and care?
Why do grown-ups not step in
Too busy or don't dare?

These children are our future
It's up to us you know
To show the way, to guide them in
Or down and down we'll go.

Most of us have made it
Because of folks who knew
To raise a child you must be strong
And tell them what to do.

To be their friend is wonderful
Commendable it's true
But they need parents more than friends
Who *live* what they should do.

You parents pay attention!
It's high time that we start
To save our children's futures
Get busy! Do your part!

...The house of cards you're building
must one day hit the ground...

Shame On You America

Slavery was the start
Of a system of exclusion
That would threaten throughout history
To bring this country to conclusion

The truth of man's equality
Can't always be kept down
All men are equal in God's sight
Red, white, yellow, black and brown

Shame on you America
You cradle of liberty
The chink in your great armor
Is denial of equality

There is no logic to your stance
To keep some people down
The house of cards you're building
Must one day hit the ground

The seeds of your undoing
Are growing all around
It's not too late to get it straight
But time is winding down

Let's start by treating everyone
With care and dignity
With equal education
And full equality

Respect for self and others
is the measure of a man...

There's More To Life Than Looking Good

There's more to life than looking good
There's character and class
The qualities in life that count
The ones that really last

Respect for self and others
Is the measure of a man
Love for people, not for things
Is part of God's great plan

Your life will be the better
If these lessons you will learn
Study them and make them yours
Life's beauty you'll discern

Look for the meaning in your life
Find your purpose, then you'll see
How rich and full of treasures
Your life on earth can be

You didn't always feel good,
you couldn't always smile...

God Bless You, Mom

I haven't always done those things
That you would have me do
But I learned vital things from you
Things you never knew

The lessons that you taught me
Your quiet gentle ways
Have brought me goodwill everywhere
And brightened all my days

The courage you displayed
When times got really tough
I learned it and it's helped me
When things have gotten rough

You didn't always feel good
You couldn't always smile
But you always let me know
You loved me as your child

Don't ever think that you're not able
you're as good as all the rest...

Give Yourself A Chance

Give yourself a chance
Don't say *I can't* before you try
Give yourself a chance
You just might kiss your woes good-bye

Give yourself a chance
Keep thinking *yes* what'er betide
The other fellow may not help,
You should at least be on your side

Don't ever think that you're not able
You're as good as all the rest
You will make it just keep trying
And always, always do your best

Don't let your gonads
own you...

Advice To A Son

My son, my dear son
I want you to be strong
I want you to be all you can
And do no person wrong

I'll do my very best
To make you proud of me
I'll teach you self-reliance
And what a man should be

The world has lots of villains
Just waiting to ensnare
Unwary, naive people
So, son you best take care

On matters of the heart
I'll just give this advice
Don't let your gonads own you
Now, walk around that twice

Don't make excuses for mistakes
Use them for what they teach
Keep growing, learning, striving
Your goals you'll one day reach

Place proper stress on money
Don't let it be your god
Raise your kids with love and care
And use the chastening rod

The strides you make in life
Are mainly up to you
Determine your direction
Then do what you must do

Always remember, the right woman
Is God's special gift to you
When you find her treat her right
She'll bring joy your whole life through

29

Though we sing not with one voice,
a common heritage we share...

Black Family Reunions

The slings and arrows of history
Tried to rip from us our hearts
But resilience of Black families
Would not let us tear apart

Through slavery and bigotry
And discrimination's lies
We've not bowed down to oppression
Desire for freedom's in our eyes

Though we sing not with one voice
A common heritage we share
And reunions of Black families
To that kinship witness bears

When Black folks come together
In the spirit of unity
There's nothing else quite like it
It's a beautiful thing to see

The energy levels soar
Conversation's loud and sweet
Families greeting families
And lots of food to eat

These reunions reconnect us
Re-linking ties that some would break
Let's stick together and maintain them
Our race's future is at stake

Is not marriage like a flower?
Can it grow without your care...

What Happened To Your Marriage?

What happened to your marriage?
Did she change or was it you?
Do you still woo and pursue her
The way you used to do?

A flower grows when watered
Once picked, needs water still
Is marriage any different?
Can it grow of its own will?

Is not marriage like a flower?
Can it grow without your care?
Can it grow, mature and blossom
If the caring isn't there?

Reclaim the magic you both shared
When marriage was brand new
It still takes what it took then
Each day live *I love You*

Happiness and sadness can't be together
cause you never see the pair...

Where Does Happiness Go?

It was here a minute ago
Did I misplace it? Has it flown?
One minute it's upon you
And the next minute it's gone

It's nothing but a tease
It won't stay for very long
It gives you joy and sweet contentment
And then sadness comes along

Happiness and sadness can't be together
Cause you never see the pair
It's either happiness or sadness
But the two are never there

It and sadness are not friends
That's very plain to see
But each one needs the other
And that's life's reality

I know you've got your problems
but brother so do I...

What Spare Change?

You say you want my spare change
What makes you think it's spare?
When time to pay my rent comes
The money's barely there

I know you've got your problems
But brother so do I
So pardon me if sometimes
I just have to pass you by

I thought there were some programs
To help those most in need
My taxes provide money
The homeless folks to feed

So remember when you see me
Looking as prosperous as I can
I'm struggling just to make it
And could use a helping hand

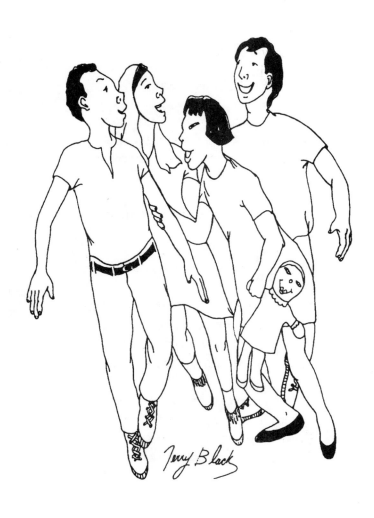

...We judge ourselves and others
by the way the outsides look...

Thoughts On Ethnicity

We know the fancy cover
Can't do justice to the book
Yet we judge ourselves and others
By the way the outsides look

What *folly* that ethnicity
Creates a gulf between
Ourselves and other people
Even those we've never seen

We judge our little puppies
By what they know and do
Too bad regarding people
The same thing isn't true

To judge a person's value
Do it as you'd judge a tree
Don't arrive at your conclusion
Till the crop of fruit you see

Ethnicity misleads you
If you use it as your gauge
America, please grow up
And begin to act your age

The glaring, simple truth is
Each is unique in his own way
Take time to get to know him
Then we'll see a brand new day

They bicker and they bicker soon
forgetting why they came...

On Committees

Committees are a useless waste
They hardly do a thing
Each member wants to run the show
Each thinks that he is king

They bicker and they bicker
Soon forgetting why they came
And the problems they're to work on
Get no action, remain the same

The way I see it, my experience
Tells me how to get it done
Just be certain your committee
Is composed of only one.

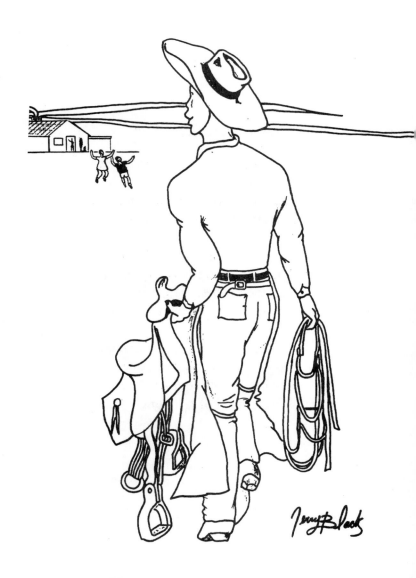

He may not always win the prize
but he'll surely give his all...

Ride'em Cowboy

At rodeos a cowboy
Gets to really show his stuff
He'll pit his skill against the rest
And hope that it's enough

He'll say his prayers before each turn
And thank the Lord for health
Then out he'll go to do his best
And perhaps increase his wealth

He may not always win the prize
But he'll surely give his all
He'll rope'em, ride'em, dog'em
To the delight of one and all

When it's all done, he'll go on home
Soak his pains and get some rest
Re-living what he did that day
He'll smile knowing he did his best

Not everybody made it that started
when you did...

44

Salute To A Graduate

Not everybody made it
That started when you did
When things got tough, some just quit
They simply ran and hid

But not you, you're a winner
You showed character and stayed
Though many got the call
Just the determined made the grade

Be sure to give a *thank you*
To those who helped you on your way
And say a prayer for those you know
Who chose not to work, but play

The foundation you are building
Will be with you all your life
If you continue building on it
You'll avoid a lot of strife

As you begin the next phase
Of a life that's on its way
Just know that I am proud of you
Today and everyday

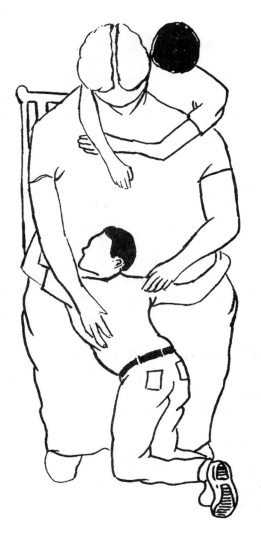

Get your head out of your butt
and think of what you're doing...

That's Reality

Some grandkids are just a heartbeat
From being in the cold
They're living with their grandma
Who's slowly growing old

Get your head out of your butt!
And think of what you're doing
Everytime you upset her
It's your own self that you're screwing

Your mom and dad are hooked on drugs
So they can't care for you
Your grandma's doing all she can
But if she dies what will you do?

No one else will take your crap
You'll be out in the cold
You'd better cherish grandma
And treat her likes she's gold

It's not your fault your folks can't cope
But grandma's all you've got
Don't kill her with bad attitudes
She cares for you a lot

She's praying for you everyday
And hoping soon you'll see
That she's the best friend that you've got
Now, that's reality!

He came to show us how to live in
peace and harmony...

The Nativity Message

The Nativity tells of Jesus' birth
All those years ago
How he came to save the souls
Of men on earth below

He came to show us how to live
In peace and harmony
To love our neighbors as ourselves
So peace on earth could be

This little child in swaddling clothes
The great example set
Of brotherhood and doing good
Tho' some have not learned yet

How simple is his message
Profound if we'd perceive
Abundant life He came to bring
To all who would believe

Trade with your own, create new jobs
or does that seem too strange?

Economics 101

It's a doomed people
Who won't trade with their own kind
Learn your economics
Try not to be so blind

You could always buy from your own
When the others wouldn't sell
Don't forget your history
Now that you're doing well

History could repeat itself
If we don't make a change
Trade with your own, create new jobs
Or does that seem too strange?

We have a chance to create jobs
In our community
Buy near to home whenever you can
It's up to you and me.

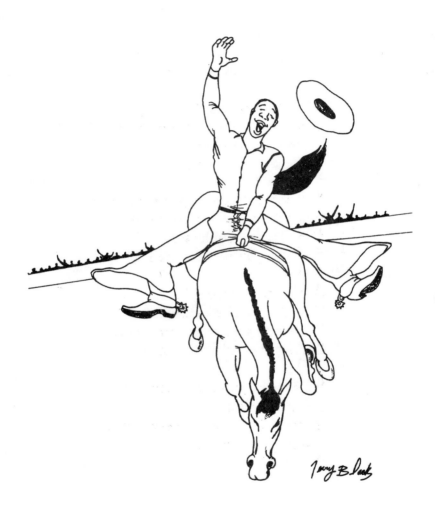

He's rugged, tough and daring
and the ladies think he's grand...

The Rodeo Cowboy

The roaring of the crowd
Is what keeps him coming back
The rodeo cowboy knows
He really has the knack

He's rugged, tough and daring
And the ladies think he's grand
They'll applaud him when he's finished
And fantasize that he's their man

He rides and ropes and bulldogs
Like tomorrow isn't there
He will sacrifice his body
For the thrill of being there

The danger doesn't scare him
He doesn't seem to mind
It's part of what he does
He daily lays it on the line

He's a rodeo cowboy
And he loves it, yessiree
He wouldn't think of trading places
With the likes of you and me

Machines don't argue, fuss or hate you
they breakdown but they don't curse...

If People Were Machines

What if people were machines
Would we be better off or worse?
Machines don't argue, fuss or hate you
They break down, but they don't curse

Family life would be the picture
Of tranquility and peace
Boys and girls would say *excuse me,*
May I, thank you, mam'am and *please*

If people acted strangely
They'd be sent in for repairs
No one would be too snooty,
No need to put on airs

When all else fails regarding people
There's no manual you can read
Nor a factory-trained mechanic
Who can give them what they need

Machines would marry for the long haul
Each would know what to expect
No silly quarrels over nothing
Children's lives would not be wrecked

Perhaps a lesson lies concealed here
If we ponder what this means
Do your duty, do your duty
Is the way of all machines

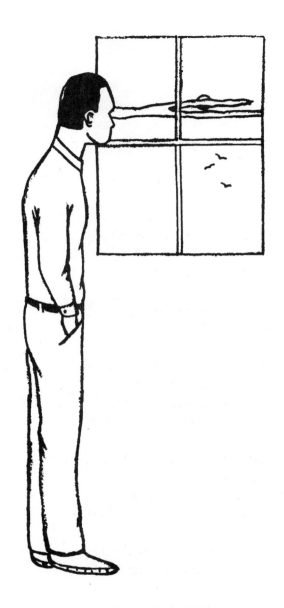

...Life will teach you if you let it,
but don't try to have your way...

Thoughts On Life

Life's a journey fraught with danger
Life's a journey filled with joy
Life will test you, maybe break you
If your faith you don't employ

More than a journey, an adventure
Learning new things everyday
Life will teach you if you let it
But don't try to have your way

Life has rules set by the Maker
Rules to guide us on our way
Rules to clearly mark the boundaries
So we'll not far from them stray

Sow and reap, *do* unto others
Love thy neighbor are but a few
For the ones who choose to break them
Life has consequences too

The rules are simple try to learn them
Live them daily and be glad
But remember one big rule is
It rains on both the good and bad.

God made you for this moment,
never doubt it, for its true...

To The Bride And Groom

May the Love that brought you together
Grow stronger with each day
And the friendship that you're building
Cause all problems to give way

May the Joy of this occasion
Never fade from memory
Side by side forever onward
You for her and her for thee

God made you for this moment
Never doubt it for it's true
For his eye is on the sparrow
Be assured He watches you

Young man you're a fine one
Strong, courageous, brave and such
This girl loves you and you love her
Always keep that gentle touch

You're both different, both quite special
What a sparkle! What a flame!
Both equipped with gifts from God
Both prepared to win life's game

Always keep your Faith in Jesus
Always know He's on your side
Call upon Him, keep Him near you
In your home let Him abide

Someday children, few or many
Will adorn your sweet love nest
Then you'll know that without question
By the Lord you have been blest

Cont'd on pg. 74

59

It doesn't really matter what *they* think
or how *they* feel...

Who Cares What *They* Say?

They say that you won't make it
They say you'll never win
But every time they count you out
You come roaring back again

It doesn't really matter
What they think or how they feel
It's your determination
That makes or breaks the deal

Set your sights on something worthwhile
Don't let nothing turn you round
If you don't let it, there is nothing
That can ever hold you down

You are the captain of your future
You are the one who holds the key
Your future's bright, go out and claim it!
There's no telling what you'll be!

One rhythmic mass of unity set free
from daily strife...

Jazz At Monterey

Every year at Monterey
Jazz takes center stage
People come from miles around
Without regard for age

September is the time of year
And Monterey's the place
Jazz becomes the medium
And we become one race

The legends of the discipline
Have played their hearts out here
And folks have come from far and near
To wave their hands and cheer

When jazz musicians get together
Something magic starts
It permeates the souls of all
It moves from heart to heart

One rhythmic mass of unity
Set free from daily strife
All eating, drinking, talking
And celebrating life!

I just want to say to you while
you're alive to hear...

I Love You, Dad

In times likes these when true commitment
Is not too often found
You stayed the course and raised your family
Thank you, Dad, for sticking around

The longer I keep living
The more I understand
The challenges a father has
He's got to be a man

And Dad, you've given all you have
And sometimes even more
You taught me courage under fire
What kid could ask for more

I just want to say to you
While you're alive to hear
I love you more than words can say
You're someone I hold dear

I love you, not because you're Dad
But just because you're you
There isn't anything on earth
I wouldn't do for you

I Love You, Dad

Kinky hair, conked hair,
menstrual cycles, what a bear!

On Turning 50: My, How Time Flies

The first 10 years of life were fun
Except when doctor slapped my buns
After that it was sucking thumbs
And eating food with only gums.

Learning to walk and talk was hip
I could move around and give parents lip
"No" and "Mama" I learned to say
And sibling bouts were the order of the day.

There were circus clowns
And friends at school
And that teacher whose kindness
Made me drool.

The next 10 years, 11 to 20
A lot went on and I mean plenty
Girlfriends, kisses, fights and stuff
Fasten your seatbelts this might get rough.

Kinky hair, conked hair
Menstrual cycles, what a bear!
Bobbing for apples, learning to swim
Watching her, watching him.

Quovadis', petticoats, necking in cars
Getting too serious, leaving with scars
Playing post office and spinning the bottle
Aroused to the max and going full throttle.

Driving permits for which we couldn't wait
Taking our partner on that first date
Carrying condoms and hoping to score
Trying to be grown up and children no more.

Doing the cha cha, the mashed potatoes
45 records, man does that date us
78 rpm's? we can't be that old
Just yesterday on campus we strolled.

cont'd on pg. 68

So get out the Ben Gay and tighten your dentures
We're much more than ready to face life's adventures
It's time to get busy and dance while we can
The next 50 years are going to be grand!

Running with gangs, the Slausons and Farmers
Running from gangs, afraid they would harm us
Prom night was different for most everyone
Romantic or frightening or just lots of fun.

The time came too soon to bid high school goodbye
"Farewell ye ole brick pile" we said with a sigh
Time to test our wings
And hope we can fly.

From 20 to 30 it was time to lock in
Time to make choices as women and men
Careers to get started or colleges too
So many choices, what were we to do.

Women burned bra's men went to fight
Killing and dying, but which side was right?
Black Panthers and hippies were the order of the day
Martin and the Kennedys taken away.

Homes, marriages, children
And even divorce
We were building, learning and slipping
As life took its course.

With credit cards we started to play
Charging and charging till we couldn't pay
What they had called credit was nothing but debt
It taught us a lesson we'd never forget.

Then came that first child, Man, were we proud!
But we'd better be careful or there'd soon be a crowd
Some were too careful, they didn't have any
And some were quite reckless, they had far too many.

But let me hasten to finish this song
Because at our age we can't sit too long
Let's see now, where was I? Oh dear, my lordy
The next 10 year span was 30 to 40.

cont'd on pg

These were some great years as best I recall
Living with teenagers was really a ball!
Radios blasting, coming home late
Not like my childhood, we got in by eight

Oh well, memory fails me
I thought I was good
It was just my mean parents
Who misunderstood.

As we approached 40, some started to slip
Hair turning gray, getting wide in the hips
Wearing eye glasses and still can't see any
Trading a good 40 for two sexy 20s.

Middle-aged crazies, most lived through it
But I must admit, some really blew it
30 to 40 and still in our prime
Going for gusto and not wasting time.

40 to 50, I'm grown now and know it!
Time to get serious lest I really blow it
Hair turning grayer if any is left
Can't shoot those baskets with hands once so deft.
We've got some new friends now
Who frequently bite us
They come uninvited
Ole Artha and Ritis.

All put together
Life's been pretty good
I wouldn't change too much
If even I could.

The friendships established and nurtured through time
Have been the main reasons that life's been sublime
Hitting big 50 don't bother us none
Cause if we're still healthy, our life's just begun.

69

Order Form

Mail order forms to: ATEA Publishing, Detroit Flanagan, 3870 Crenshaw Boulevard, Box 425B, Los Angeles, CA 90008. USA. (213) 291-4669

_____ **Please send** _____ **copy(ies) of Women & Simple Truths ($9.95 each)** $_____

_____ **Please send prints of the following poems: ($3. 95 each) 8" x 10" in size.**

Quantity	Title
_____	_____
_____	_____
_____	_____
_____	_____
_____	_____
_____	_____
_____	_____
_____	_____

Total Number Of Prints _____ **@ $3.95 each** $_____

_____ Please add my name to the ATEA Publishing Co. mailing list so I may receive information on future releases author signings or appearances in my area.

Company Name:_____
Name:_____
Address:_____
City:_____ State:_____ Zip:_____

Sales Tax: Please add 8.25% for books shipped within
           California addresses $_____
Shipping:
Book Rate: $2.00 for the first book and 75 cents $_____
for each additional book. (Surface shipping may take
3 to 4 weeks)
Optional Air Mail: $3.50 per book $_____
Prints: no additional charge for shipping $_____
Payment: Check or Money Order To: ATEA
Publishing Co.   **TOTAL** $_____

Please allow 4 to 6 weeks for delivery.

Order Today - Books or Prints Make Great Gifts!

Sample Print

All prints come combined with the facing artwork on beautiful cardstock astroparche natural, ready for matting and framing.

Don't Bring Me No Problems

Don't bring me no problems
I've got plenty of my own
If all you've got are problems
Then I'd rather be alone

I only have a little
And I worked for every bit
Don't come to me with nothing
Cause my stuff you ain't gonna git

You can be my friend
And perhaps my lover too
But moving in with nothing
Is one thing you'll never do

I'm a woman who needs love
But Mom said long ago
If you let him in with nothing
You can never make him go

So have yourself together
Or don't even look my way
I sure don't need your problems
I can hardly find my way

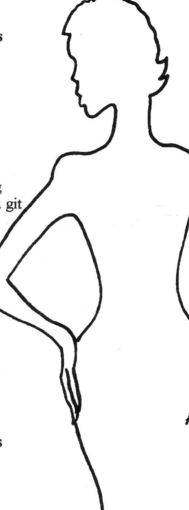

Blessed are the peacemakers...

Matt. 5:9

**And we know that all things work together for good
to them that love God..**

Romans 8:28

They'll be like you - they'll be different
They'll make you happy - make you mad
But just love them, guide them, teach them
New dimensions they will add

You will find that as you travel
New horizons you will see
Life is good! Life's a wonder!
Be the best that you can be

May your home be filled with laughter
May family ties grow ever strong
But remember, it's to each other
That you ultimately belong

So let nothing - trial nor person
Come between you from this day
God has made you, loved you, saved you
And He's with you all the way